He made

SOMETHING

BEAUTIFUL

During the last 50 years, God has been weaving a beautiful tapestry. This tapestry tells the story of the birth and growth of the dynamic, Spirit filled Panamanian church.

God uses people for special things and special times. We will forever be grateful that He allowed us to have a part of the greatest move of God we have ever experienced.

What faith we had! What passion we had! We believed God would do anything to help us win the world for Christ and we witnessed Him do that very thing!

By Janice S. Larson

Other books by this author:

El Hizo Algo Bello
(Spanish translation of this book)

Había un Indio (Spanish)

DEDICATION

This book is dedicated to everyone who had a part in the weaving of this tapestry. A tapestry, like a good story, involves more than one person. As others play a part, it becomes everyone's story and we are linked together forever.

I dedicate this book specifically to the following:

To all the Missionaries we have been privileged to work with over the years. We were inspired and challenged by your vision and dedication. You blessed and enriched our lives beyond measure.

To our Panamanian brothers and sisters – thank you for letting us be a small part of your story. Thank you for your open hearts and open arms. Your faith inspired us and together we believed God would do anything to help us win the world for Christ. We love you and we'll forever be a part of the Panama story.

To our children, Melodee, Mark, Cindee and Stephen, thank you for giving us such love and joy. We always served the Lord together as a family. Thank you for your patience, with parents who spent so much time in ministry. Each of you has your own beautiful and important part in this tapestry.

But now, Melodee and Larry Gruetzmacher, Mark and Cindy Larson, Cindee and Jason Frenn, and Stephen and Laura Larson, you, together with your children, are serving the Lord in your own callings. We love you so much.

To my wonderful husband who is the leader and visionary in our ministry. I admire your dedication to God and your desire to always do everything with excellence. It has been my extreme privilege and joy to be by your side for over 56 years. I love you with my whole heart!

A special thank you to the churches in the United States for supporting and praying for us during all these years. As our partners in ministry, you too have beautiful threads in this tapestry.

A big thank you to my granddaughter Chanel Frenn for helping edit this book.

Last but not least, I want to dedicate this book to my Lord and Savior Jesus Christ, for calling me, equipping me and permitting me to be part of this beautiful tapestry –truly knit together by His love.

TABLE OF CONTENTS

INTRODUCTION   7

CHAPTER ONE: DICK'S STORY   11

CHAPTER TWO: THE MISSIONARY CALL   15

CHAPTER THREE: PREPARING TO LEAVE   21

CHAPTER FOUR: LEARNING IN COSTA RICA   27

CHAPTER FIVE: PANAMA   35

CHAPTER SIX: EXCITING YEARS IN PANAMA   43

CHAPTER SEVEN: NEW CHURCH CONSTRUCTION   55

CHAPTER EIGHT: CATHOLIC CHARISMATICS   63

CHAPTER NINE: MINISTRY TO THE KUNA INDIANS   65

CHAPTER TEN: OUTSTANDING LEADERS ARISE   67

CHAPTER ELEVEN: TIME TO LEAVE   75

CHAPTER TWELVE: AND THE WORK GOES ON   77

APPENDIX   79

JAN'S STORY   85

INTRODUCTION

When we look at a tapestry, we see a heavy cloth, often woven by hand. The weaving produces a pictorial design of immense beauty, which sometimes tells a story. A tapestry is usually hung on a wall in a castle, museum or a home.

The warp needs to be very strong because it will be under extreme tension. The tapestry yarn just has to be beautiful, often varicolored, and available.

However, if you turn the tapestry over, it appears to be just a jumble of thread and knots going every which way. It does not look so beautiful anymore.

The Assemblies of God of Panama today, is like a beautiful tapestry, which God has woven together over the last almost 50 years. It is made of threads of many colors and different textures. It is a picture or a design of a dynamic, Spirit-filled church, taking the Gospel to its cities, its country and around the world.

Now, turn the tapestry over, and on the back, you can see how God was weaving it together and putting in a strong DNA. Each new church is an individual thread added to the tapestry. There is a thread for each Pastor that labored, suffered and faithfully served. Each Bible School, where thousands have studied, added its beautiful color to the tapestry. Each church member also has a thread, and last, but not least, are the threads of the prayers of those who have and continue to pray for this great nation.

No thread of experience is ever wasted. It includes beautiful stories of changed lives and God's faithfulness and grace.

As individuals, we too, have our own tapestry that God is weaving. If we only look at the back of the tapestry, we see the mistakes, the bad decisions, and the hurtful things that have caused damage and pain to the church and to our own lives.

However, every once in a while, God gives us a glimpse of what He is weaving and it gives us courage to continue on. We see the beauty of our journey and we are thankful because it has been so rich and full. With God in charge, He makes things beautiful

Let me take you back to how the tapestry of the Assemblies of God of Panama began. There were no Assemblies of God churches, pastors or people. It was a blank canvas and God was ready to begin the weaving.

All at the same time – although unknown to each other – three families – living and ministering in three countries – sensed the call of God to move to the country of Panama.

Panama is on both the Atlantic and Pacific oceans, where the Panama Canal connects the world, and the Bridge of the Americas connects the Americas. Although small in size, it is called the "**CROSSROADS OF THE AMERICAS**."

All three families wrote to the Missions Department of the Assemblies of God in Springfield, MO., expressing the burden they were feeling for this small country. **David and Doris Godwin** would be the first thread in the tapestry. Next **Paul and Lane Palser** would arrive. We, **Dick and Jan Larson,** would come third. We arrived in Panama on Thanksgiving Day 1968.

This is the story as we remember it. God was beginning a beautiful tapestry and He allowed us to have a part - just a tiny thread in the hand of God.

Now, almost 50 years later, we can see He truly has woven something beautiful and precious.

Hopefully others will write and add their stories as they lived them.

But to better understand, I need to tell you how God worked in our lives, about our call to work in Panama, and our life of service.

Chapter One: DICK'S STORY
(In his own words)

ADOPTED

I was born January 10, 1934 in Detroit Lakes, Minnesota to an unwed mother and placed in an orphanage. When I was three months old, a lovely lady and man came to the orphanage hoping to adopt a baby girl – to replace the baby girl they had lost at birth.

However, as they walked among the cribs looking at each baby, the lady stopped, pointed, and said, "I want to adopt this one." They took me home and I became their only child.

I'll always be thankful that I wasn't aborted. Even then, God was watching over me and placed me in a wonderful loving home.

U. S. MILITARY SENDS DICK TO PANAMA

After two years at the University of North Dakota and a broken relationship, I did not know what to do with my life. My father convinced me to enlist in the army for three years.

It was near the end of the Korean War. After basic training, everyone in my unit was sent to Korea or Germany, except for two. One was sent to Hawaii and I was sent to the Panama Canal Zone. It was November 1954.

In the Canal Zone I was looking forward to celebrating my 21st birthday on January 10, 1955. I was planning to have a big birthday bash at a bar on the famous "4th of July Avenue" in Panama City. This is the street that separated Panama City from the Canal Zone.

But, something very important happened before that party.

HIDING FROM GOD

I was raised in the Lutheran Church and taught to attend church on Sundays. Not having been to church in a long time, one Sunday morning, I went to a military chapel service in a theater on the base where I was stationed.

As I walked through the door, a guy from my unit said: "Dick, I'm so glad to see you. I will be praying for you!"

That made me so mad. Who did he think he was? Did he think he was better than me?

I walked as far back in the theater as possible and sat down in the cool, dark atmosphere, waiting for the service to start. It was a typical army chapel service.

And then, the Chaplain introduced the guest speaker for the day. He was an evangelist named Jack Wyrtzen from New York City. Now I had never heard an evangelist before and didn't know what an evangelist was, or what they did. But I was already sure I would not like it.

Jack Wyrtzen gave a testimony of deliverance from sin. He said that as an insurance salesman, he had led many people to Christ, until he finally entered the ministry full-time.

I remember very little of the sermon. I remember him talking about how his life had been changed. But then, at the end of the message, he said: "I'm going to ask you to stand to your feet if you want to ask Jesus to come into your life. We will sing a hymn and while we are singing, I want you to stand to your feet if you want to ask Christ to come into your heart. We have no counselors here to help you, so we will ask you to stand right where you are so I can pray with you."

We started to sing. In my heart I felt deep conviction and knew I should do this. My struggle became so intense that I gripped the theater seat in front of me. At the end of the first verse of that hymn, Jack said, "Don't hold on to the chair in front of you, stand up for Jesus!" I immediately dropped my hands to my lap. Wow! How could he see way back here? We were in the dark and he was far away. After that I was afraid to move.

During the second verse, I held the arms of my chair. After that verse, Jack said, "Don't hold the arms of your chair – stand up for Jesus!" I thought, how could he see me way back here in the dark?

We sang another verse. In my heart I prayed, Oh God, let somebody else stand first so I won't be the first one. At the end of the verse, Jack said, "Don't you wait for the person next to you, maybe he's waiting for you!" I thought, now he's reading my mind!

THAT DID IT

I stood – and at that moment the inner battle ceased and the peace of God flooded my heart. As we prayed the sinner's prayer aloud – I knew I was forgiven and a new life had begun. I felt so clean inside!

God had ordained my steps even before I knew Him. The U.S. army had sent me to Panama where I would find Christ and He would find me.

A few years later, God would send me (us) back to Panama, where I could return the favor and share Christ with the beautiful people of Panama. God is amazing!

MY CALL TO MINISTRY

One day in the Canal Zone – I was in the barracks listening to Jack Wyrtzen's radio program. Jack preached a message about Moses in which he said, "What is that in your hand?" I had already been sensing that God was leading me to serve Him.

When Jack said that – I looked down and realized I was holding my Bible. At that moment, it was like the Bible came alive. Not that it was physically illuminated but I just knew I was to preach the Word.

Upon finishing my tour of duty, I returned to my hometown in Minnesota. That is where Jan and I met. We attended North Central Bible College in Minneapolis, Minnesota – received the Baptism of the Holy Spirit, got married and became associate pastors at Bethel Assembly in south Minneapolis.

The Lord blessed us with three children: Melodee, Mark and Cindee. (Stephen, our fourth child was born later in Panama).

Chapter Two: THE MISSIONARY CALL

Let me tell you about our call. What is a missionary and who can describe a missionary call? The word missionary does not occur in the Bible but it comes from the Latin word "mission" which means sent. The closest word would be apostle, which describes a messenger who is sent on a mission.

It is the "Call" that compels a person to leave the comforts and security of home, family and friends to serve Christ in a foreign land.

For some, the call is dramatic and for others it is a steady growing realization that God is leading them to spend their lives taking the gospel (good news) to those who need to hear.

The "call" surrounds you - encompasses you. You breathe it. You live it. It's not a 9 - 5-day job. It encompasses your whole life. It permeates everything you do.

Acts 13:21 & 22 says, "I've searched the land and found this DAVID, son of Jesse. He's a man whose heart beats to my heart, a man who will do what I tell him." It's not usually the rich and famous who are called, but the ordinary person.

We attended North Central Bible College, in Minneapolis, Minnesota where Dick was the student body president of the missions department his senior year. In chapel, visiting Missionaries shared their stories from their countries. Our hearts were moved and broken by the need of the lost world.

WEDDING DRESS OR MISSIONARY OFFERING

Before I was married, while attending Bible College, I (Jan) remember hearing a single lady missionary from the country of Indonesia tell of the need for funds to build a Bible School in her country.

I was working about 20 hours a week and trying desperately to save enough money to buy my wedding dress. Dick and I were to marry in a few months.

I felt the urging of the Holy Spirit to give the missionary the money I had saved for my wedding dress. This I did! I am thrilled to tell you, that two months later, I found a beautiful wedding dress on sale for half price. God had provided! We were married June 7, 1958.

CALLED TO PANAMA

We were happy pastoring our first church in a suburb of Minneapolis and caring for our precious family. The church and the family were growing together. On January 9, 1964, while listening to the news, we heard that in the country of Panama, violence had broken out between Panamanian protestors and North American soldiers

Dick tuned in on his short wave radio and listened to the news. He listened - day and night, for three days. His heart was broken as he suddenly realized, that as an American he might never be able to go back to Panama. This was the first time he even knew he wanted to go back. Suddenly, we felt a nudge or a pull towards going to Panama as missionaries.

WHY US?

We have wondered many times why God called us to be missionaries. There were people better prepared than us. I had never seen an ocean, never flown in an airplane, and had trouble speaking. I Corinthians 1:26 says, "…. not many wise men after the flesh, not many mighty, not many noble, are called." But the one thing we had was a heart after God and would do anything for Him.

We did not understand that a whole new world was opening up to us, and life, as we knew it was about to change forever. With tiny steps we would learn a new culture, a new language and become part of a fabulous missionary endeavor.

PERMISSION TO BE MISSIONARIES

We contacted the Missions Department of the Assemblies of God in Springfield, MO, expressing our desire to go to Panama as missionaries. Several letters went back and forth. We received a mountain of paperwork to fill out about who we were, what we had accomplished, and our call, etc. Excitedly, we filled out the forms and waited.

Several weeks later we were invited to an interview with the Missions Committee in Springfield, MO. During the two-day drive to the interview, perhaps from stress or fear, I became sick. Yet we made it to our interview and found men of God who just wanted to make certain we were sure of our call. They approved us to be missionaries.

MUST CHOOSE ANOTHER COUNTRY

However, in Panama, there were no Assemblies of God churches or organization. The Missions Department told us we would need to choose another country where the Assemblies of God work was already strong and flourishing; a place where we could learn how to be missionaries.

We left the interview with very sad hearts. They suggested several other Central American countries from which to choose. As we began to drive home, the farther we drove, the sadder we became.

Upon arriving home, we wrote back and again asked to go to Panama. We thought, "We have been in the ministry for 2 years and certainly know how to be missionaries and how to open the Assemblies of God work in a new country." We cringe now at the audacity. We realize what a mistake that would have been. We knew nothing about opening up a new field.

The Committee wrote back and said, "NO, you can't go to Panama", but suggested we go to Costa Rica, which is the country just north of Panama. They assured us we would be close enough to enter Panama when the work was being started. We prayed, "Lord what should we do? Didn't you call us to Panama?"

THE PANAMANIAN NICKEL

We were living in Minneapolis, Minnesota. The evening before we had to make our decision, Dick drove to the corner store to buy milk. He paid with a five-dollar bill and waited for his change.

Leaving the store, he looked at the change in his hand, and right there on top he saw a Panamanian nickel. Panamanian nickels are the same size and value as the American nickel. The year was 1964 and there were only a handful of Latinos living in Minnesota. We had never seen or ever received a Panamanian nickel in our lives.

As Dick looked down at that nickel, it was as if God said to him, "If I can get this nickel all the way from Panama to Minneapolis, and into your hand on the very day that you need to make your decision, you can certainly trust me to get you to Panama when the time is right."

We immediately let the Missions Committee know we would go to Costa Rica, where we could learn Spanish, learn about the National Church, and be close enough to Panama so we could visit. They agreed! We still have that Panamanian nickel scotch-taped to our first missionary documents. God was leading us!

Chapter Three: PREPARING TO LEAVE

Rheumatic Fever

We resigned from our church in the fall of 1964, with plans to raise missionary support. We would be visiting churches and presenting our missionary vision.

Immediately after resigning, I realized I had a sore throat. A nurse in our church suggested I go to the doctor because it might lead to Strep Throat. However, I waited a few days because we had no health insurance.

Finally, Dick took me to the doctor, who seemed old to us, but was probably only in his early 60's. He told me I had the worst case of Rheumatic Fever he had ever seen and that I should go immediately to the hospital.

We explained that we were going to be missionaries and would be moving to Central America. He told us we would never get clearance to leave because of my health.

After explaining we did not have medical insurance, Dick asked if he could take care of me at home. The doctor made him promise he would make sure I stayed in bed, that he would give me Penicillin every day, check my temperature and pulse four times a day, and report back to him every three days. With that, we returned home wondering what would be our future.

Staying in bed was difficult with three little children to care for. Dick was there full time and took really good care of me.

We were praying for a miracle of Divine Healing. Several of our friends, including our dear pastor friend, Robert Hanson, came to the house that November day and prayed for me. After a few days, my pulse was back to normal, and my temperature even went below normal. Dick sincerely prayed, "Stop Lord or she's going to freeze up!"

Soon, I was well and returned to the doctor. My heart had not been damaged and the doctor said I was indeed well and he would give us medical clearance to leave for the mission field. Thank you Lord for my healing!

RAISING OUR MISSIONARY SUPPORT

We were given a personal financial budget and a work budget. It was our responsibility to find churches that would promise to send a specific amount of money each month for the following four years.

Our budget was $600 a month. It took nearly one year for us to raise that support. By having four or five services a week we were able to visit over 100 churches.

It was quite a year traveling with three young children. We rarely stayed in hotels, usually staying in the pastor's home. Melodee, who was the oldest (5 years old), remembers sharing a bed with a pastor's daughter she had never met before. (Thank you, pastors, for opening up your homes and for each meal you prepared for us).

MASTER'S DEGREE

Dick was working on his Master's degree in Communications from the University of Minnesota. It was urgent he complete the project before leaving the United States.

There were no computers in those days. As he traveled from church to church to have services – he would make use of his time and would sit in the car with a big typewriter on his lap, typing his thesis.

He finished his thesis the day before we left for Costa Rica.

PRODUCING A LP RECORD

Back in 1965, there were no CD'S or DVD'S, but we did have 33-1/3 rpm phonograph records. So we cut a long play record and titled it "The Songs of the Reaper". Our only accompaniment was a piano and an organ.

Dick and I sang duets, and even little Melodee sang a solo. We recorded it real late one night in a radio studio in St Paul, MN. When it was time for Melodee to sing, we had to wake her up, where she was sleeping on the church pew. Her little voice was so sweet.

We sold the records in our services for $3.00 each and asked people to please pray for us as they listened. When we got to Costa Rica, we used that money to purchase a piano for our home and I was able to give the children piano lessons.

SAYING GOODBYE

The train was late on that cold northern Minnesota night in January 1966. After visiting over a hundred churches, we had raised all our missionary support and shipped the 13 barrels, filled with clothes and household goods, which we would need for the next four years.

Suddenly, we heard the whistle of the approaching train, and knew it was time to say goodbye. How do you say goodbye to your parents, knowing you probably won't see them again for four years?

The grandparents held their grandchildren tightly that night. Melodee was six, Mark was four and Cindee was two.

It was the night we had dreamed about for over a year. We were starting a new life in a new country. We eagerly climbed on the midnight train and through a frosty window waved to the precious loved ones we were leaving behind. One grandmother was still holding a little doll that Cindee had left behind in our rush to board the train.

As the train pulled away from the depot, we watched from the window as our loved ones disappeared from sight. It wasn't until years later, as we were saying goodbye to our own children as they left for the mission field, that we understood the sacrifice our parents had made for us. They never complained and were so proud of us.

We traveled all night and arrived the next morning in Minneapolis. We spent the day taking care of last minute business and signing our official will.

The next morning we boarded the plane. Dick had flown on a plane before, but it was the first plane ride for the children and me. We landed in New Orleans and had our first view of the ocean. We were on our way.

The prop plane we boarded the following morning, landed at each Central American country. There was no air conditioning in the airports. Some only had roofs, so we sat in the hot, humid heat waiting to re-board the plane. There was little to eat and we were feeling hungry and tired.

Finally, the announcement came over the intercom to prepare for landing in San Jose, Costa Rica. What a beautiful sight to see the city of San Jose, which sits at four thousand feet and is surrounded by beautiful Central American mountain chains rising to the sky. The plane circled the city and found the point of entrance between the mountains. The plane landed quickly. Missionary David Kensinger met us at the airport and took us to the house that had been rented for us. Wow! We had arrived.

CHAPTER FOUR: LEARNING IN COSTA RICA

Here we are. Dick is 31 and I am 25 and we have three young children. We speak no Spanish and our most urgent challenge is to learn how to live in a new culture and to speak a new language.

Now I need to set up a household for the family and create a home where we will feel safe, and where the children will have a place to call home in the midst of a new culture. To top it off, like in many Central American families, a maid would serve as a "babysitter/maid" and sometimes even live in the house. I was to tell her what to do, how to do it, when to do it and I couldn't even speak her language. Our life as missionaries was just beginning.

LANGUAGE SCHOOL

Our first year in Costa Rica was spent learning Spanish and learning to work and think cross culturally. It was quite a year to say the least. We had classes every morning, homework in the afternoon and spent the evening with our kids. Cindee, our 2 year old, really learned to speak Spanish first because she stayed at home with the "maid" and played with our Costa Rican neighbor children.

MISTAKES MADE IN SPANISH

Dick learned Spanish quickly and after a few months he began to preach. Many words in Spanish are similar to those in English and it is very easy to get confused. In one of Dick's first sermons, he used the illustration of an ostrich hiding his head in the sand (arena). However, what he really said was that the ostrich was hiding his head in the oatmeal *(avena)*.

Another confusion or mispronunciation is the word pulpit, which in Spanish is *"púlpito"*. But, if you change the accent towards the end of the word, you end up saying *"pulpito"* which means octopus. So in church, when preaching, you had to be very careful not to say, "It's such an honor to stand behind this "sacred octopus". The Costa Rican people were so kind and they would seldom tell you what you had said wrong, but you might see smiles or horror on their faces during the sermon.

I could fill a whole book with all the mistakes we have made and continue to make in speaking and writing Spanish.

I still am so thankful to all the wonderful people of Latin America and Spain for being so kind and forgiving towards us during the early seasons of our ministry.

LEARNING AND SERVING

Only two churches in Costa Rica had pianos in those years. I remember that before I had even learned to speak or understand Spanish, I was asked to play the piano at the Assemblies of God church in Moravia, a suburb of San Jose. This church held services at the Bible School. When it was time for the service to begin, I would sit on the piano bench and someone would place a songbook in front of me, and turn the pages as the songs were announced. It was humbling, but so appreciated by the people.

After one year of language school, Dick began to teach at the Assemblies of God Bible School in Moravia. Almost every weekend, he filled the Land Rover with students. Many were already pastors of churches in different villages and towns.

He would drop them off at their homes so they could preach on Sunday morning. Then he would pick them up again on Sunday afternoon so that they could be back on time to attend classes Monday morning. Many times he would stay at one of the churches and preach. He slept on a church bench until he learned to carry a hammock with him. He would tie the ends of the hammock to the rafters in the church building. However, learning to sleep in a hammock without falling out took some experimenting.

"STOP!"

One night Dick was returning home, alone, after visiting a church in the southern part of the country. We lived in the capital city of San Jose, and to arrive home he had to cross the mountains named, "Cerro de la Muerte" (Mountain of death). These mountains were about 12,000 feet high and were usually covered with clouds. It had rained for many days and the mountain roads were full of potholes and were very dangerous.

It was nighttime and he was driving with the car windows open, and wiping fog off the windshield. Around and around the mountain curves he went as fast as he could. He caught up to a truck and followed the trucks taillights.

Suddenly, he heard the word **STOP!** It was so real, that he immediately hit the car brakes and the Land Rover came to a complete standstill. Getting out of the car, he walked to the front of the Land Rover, and saw that the heavy rains had washed away the road. Just steps away the ground disappeared. There was a drop off that went down thousands of feet. Without the voice telling him to stop, he would have driven off to his death. Following the taillights of the truck, he had not seen the washout or the temporary road going around it. He only saw the taillights straight ahead of him when the truck was back on the main road again. We thank the Lord for His protection that night!

YOUTH MINISTRY

Bible Quiz. Shortly after we arrived in Costa Rica, Dick was asked to be the Youth Leader for the country. He had never worked with youth before, so he decided to do what he had seen youth do in the United States.

He started Bible Quiz teams all over the country. Each year the theme was a different book of the Bible. He translated the materials from English to Spanish and typed it on an IBM typewriter and used a mimeograph to make copies. Soon, teams all over the country were memorizing the Word of God and quizzing with each other. At the end of the year, one team became national champions.

Speed the Light. In those years, Marcos Murillo, the Superintendent of the Assemblies of God of Costa Rica, drove a motorcycle. To visit the churches, he would cross the mountains up to 12,000 feet and then go all the way down to the ocean. Many roads were full of potholes, were narrow and very difficult to navigate. And, of course, he drove at full speed.

We worried about his safety and felt that he needed a more secure method of transportation. The Assemblies of God Youth Ministry in the U.S. have a program called Speed the Light. They raise money to purchase cars, and equipment for missionaries. Our Land Rover had been purchased by the youth and was one example of this incredible ministry.

The Costa Rican youth accepted the project to purchase a car for their Superintendent. One church planted rice and gave all the proceeds. Many people gave a day's pay. With their offerings, and a $1500 donation from the United States, we purchased a beautiful, bright red, used Land Rover.

It was at the Costa Rican National General Council, with the youth choir singing, "Onward Christian Soldiers", that the bright red Land Rover, which we had washed in the river that day, was driven up beside the tabernacle platform and presented to Superintendent Marcos Murillo. It was like a dream come true. What we had not considered was the fact that he still needed to learn to drive it. So, who would drive it back to his home? It was decided that Dick would drive the Superintendent's Land Rover, and I would drive ours. Along with all three children piled in the back, we drove several hours over the mountains and arrived safely home.

CINDEE'S LITTLE FINGER

One afternoon, Dick and I pulled into our carport with our Land Rover full of groceries. Cindee, who was 3 years old, was sitting on the top step right by the front door. Dick climbed the steps with his arms full of groceries. He entered the house and just as he was shutting the door behind him, he heard Cindee say, "No Daddy." Cindee had stuck her little finger in the crack of the door, between the wall and the door, and didn't have time to get it out before the door shut.

We quickly ran and opened the door. The tip of her finger was still attached but only hanging by a little piece of skin. Her wails filled the air as we rushed her off to the clinic, where the doctor pushed the tip back on to her finger, bandaged it up and sent her home.

We were so afraid she would bump her finger while playing, that we tried to keep her safe inside. In two days we were planning to leave the city, to stay in a tent at a church campground. This place would have no clean water to drink, nor clean water for bathing. We wondered if Cindee would be okay or if she would get an infection in her finger.

Trusting God, we left in our Land Rover, and soon into the trip we noticed her finger was starting to bleed. We stopped at a small town out in the country, and found a doctor's office. The nurse took Cindee and went off to a different room, but Dick jumped over the counter and followed close behind.

The doctor was getting ready to cut off the tip of her finger, but Dick insisted they just push it back on again, which they did. With her finger again bandaged, we left trusting the Lord to heal her.

If you could see her today, you would hardly see a mark. She even used that finger to play the flute. Cindee and her husband, Jason Frenn are Missionary Evangelists to Latin America. The Lord was merciful to Cindee and it has always been a testimony of God's love and His care for her.

LEARNING FROM OTHER MISSIONARIES

Who would we be fooling, if we didn't say that almost everything we know about missions, we have learned from other missionaries! There are too many wonderful missionaries to mention by name, but I have chosen two from Costa Rica.

David and Ruth Kensinger, our mentors:
When we arrived in Costa Rica, our mentors were veteran missionaries David and Ruth Kensinger. We first met them at our missionary interview back in our home in Minneapolis, Minnesota.

A veteran missionary can either make or break a new missionary by the way they treat them. The Kensingers were wonderful to us. They introduced us to the pastors, and took us to visit the churches throughout the whole country. Their Speed the Light Vehicle was a pickup with a camper on the back. David drove full speed on those mountain roads, with us in the back, holding on for dear life. Wow! What a ride!

From Ruth, I learned the importance of fixing up and decorating a house to make it into a home. Every detail in her house was perfect and everyone was welcome, from the most humble to the most important. Ruth made all her curtains and decorated then with ball fringe. Soon all the new missionaries had curtains with ball fringe.

I remember how Ruth's patience was greatly put to the test one day, when our Cindee, and Cindy Godwin, little girls of four years of age, got into Ruth's perfume bottles. The little girls were disciplined, but she always welcomed them back to her home. The most important lesson we learned from David and Ruth was to "love the people."

Elmer and Lee Bueno: During our third year in Costa Rica, Elmer and Lee Bueno, and their two children Chris and Kim, came from California, with the sole purpose of having a citywide crusade. They had a television ministry called "Buenos Amigos". They sang, preached and interviewed movie stars and other important people, whose lives had been transformed by the Lord.

The Buenos brought a tent called the "Air Cathedral" (Catedral Del Aire). It was a tent that used big blowers to hold it up with air. Two things needed to be done before they could inflate the tent and start the crusade, and they asked for our help.

Someone needed to go to the television station and promote the crusade and someone needed to drive the pickup and haul sawdust to cover the ground where the tent would stand. If you know us well, you can easily guess who did what. Dick dressed up in his best suit and tie and went to the television studio. And by the time I had finished driving the pickup, I was covered with sawdust from head to foot.

We learned so much about crusades by working with the Buenos. I played the accordion and the keyboard, and Dick led some of the services. Many, many people were saved and healed. Only eternity will reveal all the things the Lord did.

A great church was established out of that crusade. The next year we moved to Panama, but again were blessed to work with the Buenos. Elmer is now in heaven, but we are still friends with Lee and her children.

It was during our time in Costa Rica, that we first met **Ramiro Morris.** You can read his story later in this book.

We had three wonderful years in Costa Rica learning how to be missionaries. We will always love and appreciate the Assemblies of God leaders and people of Costa Rica, for their open hearts and kindness to us.

CHAPTER FIVE: PANAMA

THE BEGINNING

God was now opening the door for the Assemblies of God to begin in Panama. We had made several trips to Panama and already felt part of what God was going to do.

David and Doris Godwin, along with their three boys and one girl were the first of the three missionary families to move to Panama. Before moving to Panama, they started their ministry as Evangelists, and soon were ministering in Mexico. After several years in Mexico, they received their appointment as Assemblies of God missionaries and went to Costa Rica where they started a church in the city of San Pedro.

During their time in Costa Rica, they learned that the neighboring country of Panama had no Assemblies of God work. After their four years in Costa Rica, and one year visiting churches in the United States, they moved to Panama.

One of the first things they did was to rent a large house, set up a radio studio, and began daily radio programs

CHURCH PLANTING CRUSADE BEGINS JUNE 1967

After being on the radio for several months, they invited Evangelists Richard and Elva Jeffery to come and help them begin the crusade that was designed to start a new church.

They found an empty lot and put up their canvas tent with big banners saying "The Healing Crusade" (La Campaña de Sanidad Divina). Brother Jeffery preached a simple message of faith in English, and David Godwin interpreted it into Spanish.

At the end of the message, they gave two invitations. The first invitation was for salvation and everyone came forward and prayed together. For some of them, it meant praying many times, until they came to understand they were forgiven.

The second invitation was for healing, and after prayer, many people got out of their wheel chairs and walked away, leaving their wheel chairs or crutches behind. It was a true revival and many hundreds of people came to the Lord.

After many months in the tent, they found a theater that was for sale just a few blocks away. It was one of the filthiest theaters in the city, both in the pictures they projected, and in the use of the building.

The church people cleaned it up and named it "Templo Vista Hermosa". The revival continued night after night. They started an hour of teaching each night before the service, and soon began a night Bible School for those who were already feeling the call to ministry.

Those first Christians, which were born in revival, grew quickly in the Lord, and became the first wave of workers to plant more churches.

Threads of the new converts began to show on the back of the tapestry.

When the Godwins began to preach Jesus, it truly became **"SUNRISE at the CROSSROADS OF THE AMERICAS"**.

Only they can tell their story, but few have ever inspired us like the Godwins.

CANAL ZONE CHURCH

Paul and Lane Palser and their family, were the next missionaries to arrive in Panama. After pastoring churches in the United States, they went as Assemblies of God missionaries to English speaking British Guyana. There they planted a great church and produced a daily radio ministry which eventually reached thousands.

Feeling the call to Panama, they attended the Spanish language school in San Jose, Costa Rica and arrived in Panama in 1968. They came with the purpose of planting an Assemblies of God church in the Panama Canal Zone that would serve the Military and those who lived and worked for the Canal Zone.

They began by conducting Saturday night prayer meetings. This lasted for several months. During that time, they negotiated the purchase of a great piece of property, high on the side of Ancon Hill in the Panama Canal Zone. The price was only $5,000 for 4000 sq. feet. The auditorium could seat up to 150, and came with a fellowship hall that could be used as a servicemen's center.

However, while waiting to start the Canal Zone church, the Palsers visited the city of Colon, a city on the Atlantic Ocean. There they found the same kind of people they had just worked with in English speaking British Guyana.

Their hearts were touched by the tremendous need of the city. They found a large theater to rent and began services. Hundreds of people started attending and it became obvious that God was sending another great revival. This eventually became Calvary Temple of Colon.

We arrive in Panama November 1968

The church in Panama was now 1-½ years old. We had visited Panama several times to observe the progress and finally we were going to move there.

Saying goodbye to Costa Rica was difficult, but at last we were seeing the fulfillment of our dream and going to where God had called us. We arrived in Panama on Thanksgiving Day 1968.

Lord, please give us at least 10 years!

We arrived at a difficult time in Panama. In October, one month before we arrived, there was an overthrow of the Government. President Arnulfo Arias was thrown out and had to leave the country. There were soldiers with machine guns on almost every street corner. It was a time of confusion and instability. As North Americans, we knew that this could close the doors for missionary ministry. Our prayer became, "Lord, please give us at least ten years."

One year assignment

We arrived planning to minister in Panama City. However, since the Palsers were planting the new church in Colon, the greatest need was for someone to pastor the new Church starting in the Canal Zone. So we agreed to do that.

We dedicated the newly purchased building on a beautiful tropical Sunday morning in 1969. Dr. G. Raymond Carlson, Superintendent of the Assemblies of God in the USA was the dedication speaker. We loved working with the service men and their families, and those who lived in the Canal Zone. They so appreciated having a church just for them. If we hadn't just spent a year learning Spanish, and felt called to the Spanish world, we would gladly have stayed on forever as their pastors.

During that year, we went to the Panama City church one night a week to teach in their Bible School. Another night, we would take the train that went from one side of the country to the other (40 miles), to the city of Colon, to teach in their Bible School or even minister in their services.

MARK IS STRUCK BY A CAR

Although ministering in the Canal Zone, we were not permitted to live there. We lived on the fourth floor in a high-rise apartment in Panama City. Our dear missionary friends, the Godwins, lived on the seventh floor. Our children were best friends. They would frequently cross a busy street to go to a store for candy or to get a haircut.

Our son Mark was eight years old at the time and one day, I don't know why we let him do this, he was crossing that busy street by himself and was hit by a car. He was knocked unconscious and lay there in the middle of the street. It was a miracle he was not hit by other passing cars.

Thankfully, the driver of the car that hit him stopped and picked him up. He put him in the back seat of his car and took him to the Santo Tomas hospital. When they arrived at the hospital, Mark woke up enough to tell the nurse his telephone number. It was midmorning when I received a call from the hospital saying my son was there and that I was needed immediately.

Dick was ministering on the Rio Tigre San Blas Island, and wouldn't be home until the following day. There was no way I could contact him. I quickly found someone to stay with the other children and rushed to the hospital. I found my son. He lay there with a huge lump on his head and a broken leg. The doctor told us the bone near his hip had been broken, and his leg would need proper care.

As I waited to take care of the paperwork for admission to the hospital, a Panamanian lady came over and spoke to me. Her husband was a Colonel in the United States Air Force. She urged me to move Mark to the military hospital in the Canal Zone. She felt he would get better care there. I explained, that although we were Americans, we did not have permission to use that hospital. However, she continued insisting I do so. Finally, I called and was able to make the arrangements and we moved him to "Gorgas Hospital".

It was a wonderful hospital and I'll always be grateful that Mark could be there. They operated and put a pin in his leg. He stayed in the hospital, in traction for seven weeks. Then he was put in a body cast from his feet to his chest, for seven more weeks, and we were able to move him home.

We were still pastoring the church in the Canal Zone. The church was built on a hill. There were approximately 40 steps leading up to the building. Every Sunday, we would place Mark, wearing his body cast, on a reclining lawn chair. With my husband Dick on one side and me on the other side, we would carry him up those forty steps. We would stay at the church all day Sunday so as not to have to do it twice in one day.

He eventually healed just fine and has had no trouble with his leg. Sometimes we wonder why things happen, but God always brings something good out of the bad.

Later in this book, I will tell how God used my conversation with this Panamanian lady to supply the financing for the construction of the new Panama City church building.

RETURNING TO THE UNITED STATES

After three years in Costa Rica, and one year in Panama, it was time to return to the United States to visit and report to our missionary supporting churches.

The missionaries who were to take our place in the Canal Zone church were still raising their financial support and not yet ready to come. Our dear friends, Bob and Monzelle Hanson, Pastors of Bethel Assembly in South Minneapolis, MN, came with their children, at their own expense, to fill in as pastors of the church. They did a fantastic job! That was the spring of 1970.

Chapter Six: EXCITING YEARS IN PANAMA

In January 1971, we packed our suitcases to return to Panama. We were given a brand new car, purchased by the young people from the Assemblies of God churches in Minnesota.

So, with three children in the back seat, and with me being four months pregnant and sick, we left Minnesota to drive the 4000 miles to Panama. In those days, there were few freeways, and I remember going round and round the hairpin turns through Mexico, all the way through Central America, until we finally arrived in Panama.

WAIT FOR US FOR WE ARE YOUR LEADERS!

The Godwins needed to leave for their year of visiting churches in the United States, and it seemed natural for us to take their place as pastors of this growing dynamic church. The Panama City church, named "Templo Vista Hermosa" was now 4 years old and making a great impact on the city.

The theater, now converted into a church, could seat over 500 people, with two services on Sunday, and services Tuesday, Wednesday, Thursday, and Friday nights. There were approximately 20 outstations (preaching points) all around the city, which met on Saturdays.

The Church had also started a Bible School that had classes three nights a week. During the evening service, David would teach, while Doris led the worship. Then, Doris would teach, while David preached. Remember, this was the first Assembly of God work in

Panama and they were doing their best to get workers and pastors trained.

David Godwin had two or more daily radio programs. Monday evenings were the only free times of the week. Doris Godwin almost lost her health. Unless you have been part of a revival, it's difficult to understand how exhausting the work can be. The Assemblies of God of Panama is the great work it is today because of the Godwin's love and dedication.

Following the Godwins, as pastors of this tremendous church, was like jumping on a speeding freight train and holding on for dear life. We did our best to keep things going, although our personalities and gifts differ from those of the Godwins.

At first, I know I was a disappointment to some of the Panamanians. Although I played the organ, piano, accordion, and helped lead the worship, I was not a public speaker.as was Doris Godwin. So many times I have asked God why He didn't gift me in that way. Almost every Panamanian has the ability to stand up in front of people and speak or say a poem.

So, to those who ever felt that way, please know I did my best by using my God given musical gifts and great love for the people.

In this hot and humid church building, with no air conditioning, Dick would be very tired after preaching and praying with people around the altar. Many nights he would sneak out the back door, but I would stay and visit and love on the people.

Dick continued with the daily radio programs and also added others. He used all methods of communication, including television programs three nights a week.

BIRTH OF OUR SON STEPHEN

Our son Stephen (Esteban) was born in Panama, on July 5th, 1971. Every night, I played the organ for the church services. We had an Evangelism Team from Minnesota there the week Stephen was born. We had been given permission for him to be born at Gorgas hospital in the Canal Zone, where Mark had been hospitalized for seven weeks.

The day he was born, there was a funeral at the church for one of our former board members, and I was to play the organ.

However, about an hour before the funeral began, I began to have labor pains. Dick quickly drove me to the hospital and left me so he could officiate at the funeral.

Thankfully, he got back to the hospital on time to be there for the birth, although in those days the father was not permitted in the delivery room.

What a joy it was the day Stephen was born. He became the family project. His sisters and brother all wanted to take care of him, especially at church, where they could sit in the air-conditioned office with him. The whole church loved him and in Panama he is still known as "The Panamanian".

THE DYNAMIC YOUTH GROUP

The youth of the church were on fire for God. Many were studying in the Bible School and preparing for the ministry. The youth group was called Koinonia, which is a word from the original Greek New Testament, which means fellowship. For many weeks, when they were together, they would only talk about the things of the Lord - nothing else.

In those first years, youth evangelism teams came from the United States and taught our young people how to evangelize. Soon the Panamanian youth were witnessing in their schools. One school had an election for student class president and so many kids wrote in the name "Jesus" for candidate, that He won the election!

Every Saturday, the youth would head to soccer fields where teams were playing. During the intervals, they would go out on the field, and share their testimonies of what the Lord had done for them. Many times, whole soccer teams knelt in prayer to accept the Lord as their Savior.

We had many wonderful youth leaders and youth pastors. I hesitate to name them lest I forget some. They know that we love them and thank the Lord for their lives and their ministry.

THE YOUTH CHOIR

My greatest joy was directing the youth choir. Dick helped me a lot and so did Melodee, as she got older.

There were approximately 20 to 30 youth in the choir. We started by singing two-part harmony. Some of the youth really couldn't sing very well, but their enthusiasm carried them a long way.

We made several uniforms for the choir. At first it was long skirts and white blouses for the girls and white shirts and dark pants for the guys. One year, all the guys had white pants and red shirts. For very special occasions, we used tuxedo shirts and fancy dresses.

We even had the privilege of ministering at the prison on Coiba Island.

INVITED TO SING IN VENEZUELA

Missionary Juan Romero was a frequent guest at the church. We lovingly called him, the "Happy Mexican" ("El Mejicano Alegre"). Brother Juan wrote and sang all his own music.

One Sunday, Juan Romero was ministering at the church. After hearing the youth choir sing, he was very impressed, and publicly invited them to travel to Venezuela, to sing in a big conference where he would be singing and Nicky Cruz would be speaking. (*Nicky Cruz had been saved from drugs and gangs in New York – under David Wilkerson and wrote the book "Run Nicky Run"*)

Of course, the choir with enthusiasm said, "Yes, we want to go" and after all the excitement had settled, we started to think of how we could afford to get there. In those days, a round trip ticket from Panama to Caracas, Venezuela cost $200. So we figured that $200 times 30 kids would be about $6,000.

These young people didn't have that kind of money, but there was one thing they did have, they had tremendous faith. They said, "God wants us to go and sing to thousands of people and He will help us get there."

They started to pray, and while praying, they would get an idea. They called the Panamanian government to see if they had a plane to fly them to Venezuela, but the government's plane was broken.

They had lots of ideas on how to raise funds, but none worked out. Every day they were at church praying. Finally, it was the week of the conference. On Sunday of that week, Dick was leaving for Venezuela because he needed to be there early for some meetings. The choir needed to arrive on Friday night.

As Dick left for the airport, he remembers praying, "Lord don't let the youth choir be too disappointed if they don't get to Venezuela." He reminds me now that he is ashamed of having such little faith.

On Monday, some of the youth choir told their families, (many from unsaved homes), that they were going to Caracas, Venezuela. They explained that they did not know what day they were leaving, and were taking their suitcases to church just to be ready.

They would pray all day and then at night they would go home. This went on until Friday afternoon. It was the last day to get tickets, so part of the choir decided to go to the Pan American airline office and ask for tickets.

They entered the office, and said to the ticket agent, "We need to fly to Caracas, Venezuela today." They were told there were only 16 tickets left on the evening flight. In that moment, the young people decided that half the choir would go, and the other half would need to stay behind and pray.

They said, "Okay, please get the tickets ready and while you are doing that, could we meet with the director of the agency?" They were led to the director's office, where they started to sing and share their testimonies with him. They told of being set free from drugs and how God had transformed their lives. Soon they saw tears in the eyes of the director and he said to them, "**I don't know why, but I'm going to give you these 16 tickets and write it off as publicity.**

When they got back to the church, I had the difficult job of choosing who would travel and who would stay behind and pray for the group. Thankfully, there were no hard feelings. For these kids it was all ministry.

That night, Melodee and I flew with the choir to Caracas, Venezuela. When we got off the plane, Dick was waiting for us. He told me later, that when he saw the young people get off the plane, they walked like kings and queens. God had responded to their faith! And yes, they ministered to thousands. How great is our God!

SINGING CHRISTMAS TREE

We wanted to do something special in the church for Christmas. Churches in the United States were presenting what they called "The Singing Christmas Tree" which inspired us to do so as well. Inside our church building, down at the front, we built an 18-foot tall wooden structure in the shape of a Christmas tree. We decorated it with Christmas decorations and lots of greenery.

We decided to videotape the presentation for television. In order to tune out the nearby street noises, we closed all the windows and doors. The youth choir took their places in the tree structure and the cameras began to roll. There was only one problem. It became stifling hot on that tropical Panamanian night. The church was not air-conditioned and the heat was hardly tolerable.

Each member stood in place within that large structure and began to sing. Suddenly, we heard a terrible cracking noise. It had gotten so hot that one of our larger young men, named "Chico", who was standing about six feet off the floor, fainted. He fell, breaking a chair in the front row of the church. Luckily, the cameras were not focused on him. The choir continued singing and most didn't even know what had happened until we finished the program. And, Chico was not hurt.

CARNIVAL

In those years, the celebration of "Carnival" in Panama was the second largest in the world, right after Rio de Janeiro, Brazil. So much evil went on during Carnival that many churches of other denominations, took their young people and retreated to the interior of the country.

The DNA of the Panama City Church was pure evangelism. So without hesitation we decided to create a float representing our church and put it in the Carnival parade.

We ordered over a million tracts from Light for the Lost (the literature program of the A/G in the United States). The young people rolled each tract in cellophane and tied them with rubber bands. This way, they could throw them into the crowds of people along the parade route.

We rented a large flatbed truck, decorated it with signs that said, "Jesus is the Answer", "Have Faith in God", and the name of our church "Catedral de Vida". We put the tracts in barrels on the truck, and the youth choir sat on the barrels until it was time to take out more tracts.

We recorded the youth choir singing and put a sound system on the truck. For their protection, we put the girls in the center of the truck, surrounded by the guys. When our float (decorated truck) got in line for the parade, there was another truck behind them with a band playing Latin Cha Cha Cha music. We were afraid no one would even hear our choir.

The parade started and people along the parade route said they could really hear the choir but barely hear the band. People were eager to receive the tracts. We had strategically placed church people along the parade route ready to minister to people who received the tracts.

When the parade was over, the choir returned to the church to share in the evening service. It was thrilling to hear their experiences and their testimonies of sharing Jesus in the middle of Carnival!

The next day, on the back page of the Panamanian newspaper, there was a picture of our float with a caption that read, "The Church shows the real Joy of Carnival.

CANTATA HALLELUJAH

Bill and Gloria Gaither had just written a vocal composition (cantata) called Hallelujah. We wanted to present it as an evangelistic outreach but it had not yet been translated into Spanish. So, Dick with the help of others translated it. As far as we know, our youth choir was the first to ever present it in Spanish.

To help them learn the music, I sang the melody into a cassette, and each soprano took a cassette home and memorized their part. We did the same for the altos and then the tenors. We were only able to learn three-part harmony, never quite making it to the bass part. We knew that once they learned their part they would never forget it.

It was for this Cantata that we made beautiful long dresses for the girls and gave the men tuxedo shirts and dark pants. We were in our new church building by then and everything was so beautiful. We presented the concert several times and each time many people gave their hearts to the Lord.

THE TELEVISION PROGRAM

We were always seeking new ways to reach people for Christ. So, we decided to begin a five-minute television program that would play three nights a week. The program aired at 11:45PM, right before television went off the air for the night (yes, it really went off the air at midnight). We wanted to reach people who were restless and couldn't sleep. We prayed they would watch the program and find Christ. Our program was called **"La Catedral de Vida" – (The Cathedral of Life).**

The Youth Choir sang on many of the programs. We would tape their singing in advance by putting the best singers closest to the microphones so their voices could be heard. For the taping of the actual program, they sang without microphones. (Lip-Sync). Their smiles and enthusiasm, and yes their voices, ministered to thousands of people.

One morning, my husband received a telephone call asking him to come immediately to the Social Security Hospital. He went, expecting to find someone on his or her deathbed. Instead, he found a man dressed and ready to leave the hospital.

The man told how he had come to the hospital with a rare form of incurable cancer. But one night, when he could not sleep, he watched our television program. At the end of the program, he knelt next to his bed in the hospital and prayed to accept Christ into his life and ask for healing. The following day, the doctors tested him again and his sickness was all gone. He was going to leave the hospital and wanted to share with us his testimony.

Because of the television program, we received many testimonies of changed lives and many, many visitors at the church.

THE SINGING DEWEYS

God sent us many ministers and evangelists from various countries, to bless the work in Panama, and each contributed to the growth of the church.

Evangelists Levoy and Cleon Dewey and their daughters Cindy and Susanne, came from Nashville, Tennessee to Panama almost every year. Tim Dewey, brother of Levoy, and his wife Sheryl, came with them. Their first visit was to the Canal Zone Church in 1969. They were musical evangelists with the Assemblies of God and sang and played many musical instruments.

Even though they sang in English, we invited them to minister in our church in Panama City. They came at their own expense, sometimes having to borrow money from their bank for the trip.

They were a great inspiration and blessing. Often they left musical instruments behind to help those, especially the young people, who wanted to serve the Lord musically.

Their generosity reached all the way to the San Blas Islands. There they built a building for the Assemblies of God church on the Island of Rio Tigre. Levoy's mother and father even purchased a used baby grand piano for our church in Panama City.

The Deweys became our close friends and 28 years ago, their oldest daughter Cindy married our oldest son Mark. We have spent many holidays together and we love them dearly.

Chapter Seven: NEW CHURCH CONSTRUCTION

It didn't take long to realize we would need a larger building for the growth of the congregation. We started looking for property on major bus lines. Almost everyone rode the city buses to church. At first, there were only three cars in the congregation, and one was a taxi. Under the leadership of the Godwins, the church had started a building fund where they had approximately $5,000 in savings.

One day, our Youth Pastor, Lowell David (you can read his story later in this book) came into the church office and said, "I've found the perfect land for the new church building." He had discovered a large parcel of land located where several of the best bus lines crossed, "La Carretera Transistmica" and "Via Fernandez de Córdoba." In the middle of the land was a small house surrounded by weeds.

PLANS DRAWN UP

We began to dream about the kind of building we needed. It was so real that in our minds we could see it already built. Dick could see the platform and the pulpit where he would stand and preach. He envisioned the people coming to the altar, accepting the Lord, and being healed.

The architect drew up plans for a 1200 seat sanctuary, plus a three story educational building for Sunday school. One evening, we took the church board to see the property. We walked all around the land, praying the Lord would give us favor with the owner.

FINANCING PROMISED

Dick spoke to a bank about financing and they agreed to give us a loan to purchase the property. The owner of the property was a lady from Spain. She accepted our offer, which led to our down payment of $5,000. She gave us 30 days to get the rest of the money.

Going back to the bank, Dick told them he was ready to sign the loan agreement and receive the money. The president of the bank looked at him and said, "I'm so sorry Reverend, but our bank just changed its policy and we no longer make loans to churches." Dick looked at the bank president and simply replied, "You think you are sorry? I now must go to the church and tell them their new pastor has just lost all the money they have saved in four years."

Dick went back to the church and explained what had happened. The board and the church people were wonderful. There was no criticism. Instead, they put their trust in the Lord and began to pray.

Immediately, we began to contact bank after bank to get a loan. The 30 days passed and the owner agreed to give us 30 more. We hoped to get financing from the United States, but that didn't work out. Finally, after 180 days, the owner was so frustrated and angry with us that she said, "I have given you plenty of time. Now you need to know that I will never sell you this property."

Dick hung up the telephone after talking to her and instead of being discouraged, he sat and laughed and laughed and said, "Won't she be surprised when no one else buys it until we get our money."

DIVINE MEETING

Remember the story of when a car hit Mark and I met the Panamanian lady who encouraged me to get him into Gorgas Hospital in the Canal Zone? Well, one morning, I just "happened" to be down at the church and a lady came to our office, wanting to sell us some property across the street. She sold real estate.

When we saw each other, we realized we had met before. I immediately recalled her help when we were choosing a hospital for Mark. Dick explained that the property she wanted to sell wouldn't work for us and that we had already found property, but couldn't get financing. To make a long story short, her brother was the President of Banco de Bogota (Bogota Bank) and she felt sure he would be willing to help us.

Dick arranged an appointment to see the president of the Bank. As he walked into the president's office, unrolled the plans for the new building, and placed them on the president's desk, he could sense the presence of the Holy Spirit. After only a few minutes, he not only had the financing for the property, but also was given financing to start construction of the building. Wow! Again, God had honored the faith of the Panamanian people.

CONSTRUCTION BEGINS

These were exciting days as the foundation was laid and the walls went up. Construction teams from the United States came to help us. One team was from our home church, Emmanuel Christian Center in Minneapolis, Minnesota, led by Pastor Mark Denyes.

Day after day they worked in the hot sun and it was an awesome sight to see how fast they laid bricks. The beautiful columns went up across the front of the outside of the building, and also a balcony that could seat 500 people.

BACK TO THE TENT

Our present church building, the converted theater, had been sold and we needed to move out. However, our new building was not yet ready and wouldn't be for several months. We needed to find a different place to meet.

So, we got creative. We took the old tent out of storage (the one used to start the church in 1967) and put it on a large vacant lot, along a busy highway, a mile from our new property. The tent was very old, so much so, that you could see the stars at night through the holes.

I wish you could have seen how we had Sunday school on Sunday mornings. Inside the tent, we had several adult classes going on at the same time. Outside the tent, under the trees or anywhere you could find a little shade, were about a dozen classes for children and young people. They sat on the grass or on anything they found to use.

We expected to only be in the tent for a few months, but construction took longer than expected, and we used the tent for eleven months. However, during this time many people came to Christ.

A whole gang came and accepted Christ. Out of that gang many became pastors. Two sisters, Anita and Carmen were saved. I will tell more of their story as part of the Catholic Charismatic Story.

CRITICISM

We began to hear rumors of criticism from other church denominations about the large church building being built. Words like, "The Larsons are building their own kingdom." When we had to move back into the tent for eleven months, while waiting for the building to be finished, it was rumored that we had run out of money and couldn't finish the building. However, it's important to understand that between the years 1971 to 1975, only one A/G church in Central America was larger than ours, and that was the Evangelistic Center in El Salvador, pastored by missionary John Bueno.

And it is true. It was a large dream. By working with other missionaries and experiencing revival, we had learned to think big and believe that God does do great things. And the day came when the congregation joyously marched from the tent to the new church building. Everything was for the honor and glory of God!

EXTREME SACRIFICE

Almost all of the money to build the new church building came from the very generous Panamanian people. They gave and gave and gave. One night in church, Dick noticed a lady take something out of her ear and put it in the offering plate. He saw this happen several times.

He asked the assistant pastor what the ladies were doing. The pastor explained that when they left home to come to church, they wouldn't carry a purse for fear of thievery. They would take two coins with them. They put one coin into their ear to save for return bus fare home and the other coin was used immediately for their bus fare to church.

Many nights, they would take the coin out of their ear and put it in the offering. For these women it meant walking home, sometimes through the torrential tropical rains. The church building was built on the extreme sacrifice and love of the Panamanians for the work of the Lord.

PROTECTION FROM RAIN

In Panama it rains approximately 100 inches a year. How could our church survive in a tent full of holes and not be rained out? Many a Sunday morning, the storm clouds gathered, but they only came so close to the tent. It would rain all around the tent, but only on the last Sunday morning, before moving to the new building, did it ever rain on us. It was as if the Lord said, "See how I have protected you!"

NAME CHANGE

The new church building was no longer in the Vista Hermosa area and it was necessary to change the name. We decided to use the name of the television program and so we changed the name of the church to **CATEDRAL DE VIDA** (Cathedral of Life).

DEDICATION OF NEW BUILDING

We used the building many months before it was ready for dedication. Laying boards across cement blocks made temporary benches. I designed and sewed a beautiful gold velvet curtain that went from one side of the platform to the other. We installed a motor to lift it.

We'll always remember the night that Raquel, a young lady from the choir, began to sing while the curtain lifted. But, something went wrong with the motor, and the curtain only lifted part way. All we could see were her legs until some people climbed behind the platform and lifted the curtain manually. Raquel and the choir just kept singing during all of this confusion.

Our Executive Director of World Missions in the United States, Rev. Philip Hogan, came to be our dedication speaker. The date was January 18, 1976. Missionary Juan Bueno was also there.

What a day of rejoicing as the beautiful new 1200 seat sanctuary and three floor education building was dedicated to the Lord. The congregation assumed approximately 85 percent of the cost of the new facility. Missionary builder Gordon Weden served as overseer of the project.

A special highlight of the dedication was the presentation of a $1,000 missionary offering from the church, designated to help in the evangelistic thrust in the country of Egypt. Commenting on the gift, Brother Hogan said, "Now I know for sure that this is a New Testament church!"

One other very important thing happened that day and you will read about it later in this book when I mention **Gregorio Campos**.

Chapter Eight: CATHOLIC CHARISMATICS

These were the years that the Holy Spirit was moving in Notre Dame, a Catholic University in the United States. Many people were being filled with the Holy Spirit inside the Catholic Church and also in other denominations.

During the eleven months we were in the tent, two teenage sisters came and were radically saved. They attended the services night after night, until one night their parents came and physically removed them from the service.

Sharing their Faith

The girls, Anita and Carmen, attended a large Catholic High School. After finding Christ, they wanted to share their new experience with their friends. Eventually, some parents were curious about the changes in their children's lives. So, Anita and Carmen went to the Mother Superior and asked permission to share with the parents of their friends. The request went all the way to the Archbishop of Panama.

They invited Herminia Villareal, our church secretary, to go with them to the meeting with the Archbishop. They knew their lives had been transformed, but as new Christians it was difficult to explain. Dick told Herminia she should go with them, but first she should tell the Archbishop that she was a member of the Cathedral of Life (La Catedral de Vida) church and a minister with the Assemblies of God.

They went and received permission to have the meetings, but under strict supervision. Instead of meeting in the school, they were given permission to use a Catholic church one night a week.

The first meeting was well attended. Eventually it grew to the point of 2,000 attending. This became a catalyst that began the Catholic Charismatic outpouring in Panama. The Catholic Church was enriched. However, some people left the Catholic Church and started several Assemblies of God churches.

DINNER WITH THE ARCHBISHOP OF PANAMA

We were invited to a home where we had the privilege of meeting and sharing a meal with Archbishop McGrath, leader of the Catholic Church of Panama. He knew of our church and part of the conversation was about how his churches were starting to tithe because of the influence of the Charismatics.

MIDNIGHT MASS

A Christmas we will always remember in Panama was the year our choir was asked to sing in the "Misa Del Gallo" midnight mass at a prestigious Catholic Church. This invitation came because of our impact through the Catholic Charismatics.

Midnight Mass is the service held at midnight on Christmas Eve. We were given permission to minister in both song and testimony. The youth choir started to sing Christmas songs, interspersed with testimonies of changed lives. We closed the program singing the song, "There's room at the Cross for you." The Spirit of the Lord was so strong in that Catholic Church that night. It was a great opportunity to share our Lord Jesus Christ with so many!

CHAPTER NINE: MINISTRY TO THE KUNA INDIANS

RAMIRO MORRIS – KUNA INDIAN

Ramiro Morris is a Kuna Indian born on the San Blas Island, Rio Tigre. About 50 of the 365 San Blas Islands are inhabited by the Kuna Indians. They are a very colorful people both in spirit and in culture.

When a Kuna woman marries, her husband comes to live as part of her family. The woman inherits the money in her family and commonly is seen wearing huge amounts of gold around her neck.

When Ramiro was ten years old, his father took him to Costa Rica, where a friend raised him. He came to know the Lord in a crusade held by missionary David Godwin. We first met Ramiro at the Bible School in Costa Rica where he was studying for the ministry. To pay for his tuition he served as the cook of the school. His smile and love for the Lord was contagious.

While God was calling the first three missionary families to work in Panama, He was also calling Ramiro to return to the island where he was born and to preach to his own people.

Ramiro is a true pioneer and has suffered much in his ministry. He planted an Assemblies of God church on Rio Tigre. He and his wife Priscilla buried two children on the island but have continued to faithfully follow the Lord. Ramiro's favorite phrase is, "Everything was the plan of God."

Ramiro would come and visit us in our apartment in Panama City. He was always welcomed as one of our greatest friends. One time he brought three teenage

Kuna Indians with him. It was their first time to leave the island. They had never been in an elevator. I wish you could have seen their expressions, when after entering the elevator on main floor, a few seconds later they stepped out on the eighth floor, where they could see the whole city.

You can read his inspirational story in the book I have written called **"Había un Indio"** - the Story of Ramiro Morris. (Available on Amazon).

Chapter Ten: OUTSTANDING LEADERS ARISE

As I have mentioned, the work in Panama began in a real revival. It was a work of faith. Faith was preached night after night and God confirmed His word with signs and wonders, and miracles.

In almost every service, and we had five or six services a week, people would come and give their hearts to the Lord.

Evangelism was part of their DNA. Their goal was to fill their city, their country and the whole world with the knowledge of the Lord.

BIBLE SCHOOLS

David and Doris began the first Bible School, which was held in two classrooms above the converted theater, Templo Vista Hermosa. Eventually, veteran missionary Ralph Williams moved to Panama to serve as Director for the Bible School.

When our new building "Cathedral of Life" (Catedral de Vida) was finished, part of the upper floor was used for the Bible School. We thank the Lord for teachers like Mona Grams (now Shields) and Judy Johnson (now Kosack) and many, many others.

When Ralph Williams needed to return to the United States, God called Larry and Dorothy Cederblom to leave the Dominican Republic and move to Panama to become the new Directors of the Bible School. They took it to a new level. They eventually built a three-story Bible School building in a different location. Under their supervision many more Bible Schools were opened all over the country. It can be said that they helped to train almost all the workers in Panama. They lived in Panama for many years after the rest of us had moved on. Their thread can be seen in the tapestry for all the leaders they helped to train.

Outstanding workers came out of the revival and added their thread to the beautiful tapestry being woven. I wish I could mention every-one of them and tell you of all the outstanding things they have done for the Kingdom.

I wish you could hear the stories of lay people in Panama. Some serve the Lord in government and in different parts of society. God's people are everywhere and their threads are making a beautiful pattern in God's tapestry. They are true men and women of faith.

Let me list just a few.

LOWELL DAVID: FIRST PANAMANIAN SUPERINTENDENT OF THE ASSEMBLIES OF GOD

His story could perhaps be summed up in four simple words: "from mechanic to Superintendent." We were the new pastors of the "Templo Vista Hermosa" church in Panama City and Lowell David was the Youth Pastor.

He found the property for the new church building. The call of God was strong on him and he was a very dynamic young man! He spoke both English and Spanish.

One day Lowell came to Dick and said he wanted to start a new church in "La Chorrera", a town about 30 km southwest of Panama City. It seemed like a good idea and Dick suggested he invite Evangelist Richard Jeffery to come and help him. (Jeffery was the Evangelist that had helped Godwins start the first Assemblies of God church in Panama.) However, Lowell wanted to start right away, so we found the old tent and put it up on a good lot. Invitations were handed out and the youth choir went every night for about two weeks to sing.

It was a difficult place and for various reasons, the crusade was not a complete success. The tent was eventually taken down and Lowell went back to being a mechanic (for a short time). However, out of this endeavor, a man named **Gregory Campos** got his start in the ministry.

In a few months, Lowell, with the help of Evangelist Richard Jeffery, started a new church in the city of San Miguelito. They started on a vacant lot where many murders had taken place. The crusade was open air, with just a roof over the platform. Richard Jeffery would play his accordion, trying to get people to come to the service. One night, seeing several people walking on the other side of the property, Jeffrey called out, "Are any of you deaf?" A man pointed to someone and shouted back, "Yes, he is!" Jeffery got them to come to the platform. He prayed for the deaf man and asked him questions, which the man was able to hear and answer. The man was healed and could hear clearly.

The testimony of the deaf mans healing, quickly spread and soon they had a crowd attending the crusade. That is how we remember it, but Brother Lowell can tell you much more about the beginning of the church in San Miguelito.

Out of this endeavor, a man named **Edwin Alvarez** was saved. Eventually, Edwin started a crusade under a tin roof. This grew and is now the largest Assembly of God church in Panama: "Comunidad Apostólica Hosanna."

When the Assemblies of God of Panama was organized, Lowell David became the first Panamanian Superintendent. He is the longest serving Assembly of God Superintendent in Latin America. He and his wife Odilia have done a superb job in leading and establishing churches in almost every city in the country of Panama. Untold threads have been added to the tapestry during their ministry.

GREGORIO CAMPOS: "THE LITTLE PIECE OF PAPER"

First Panamanian Pastor of the Panama City Church - Cathedral of Life

Gregorio was a Christian, but he was so busy making a living that he didn't have much time for serving God. His wife, Doris, and their daughter would attend the Panama City Church, Templo Vista Hermosa on Sundays. Doris would continually invite Gregorio to attend, but he worked 6 days a week and wanted to rest on Sundays.

It was Sunday, New Year's Eve, December 31st, when he decided to attend the Sunday morning service. Missionary David Godwin was still the pastor and the title of his sermon that morning was, "What is keeping you from serving God?"

At the end of the message, little pieces of paper were handed out to everyone and Pastor David said, "Write down on this piece of paper what is keeping you from serving God. Then, bring your paper and burn it in the flames from the candles on the altar."

Gregorio wrote down, "My two trucks." He went to the front, burned the little piece of paper, walked out of the church and forgot all about it.

NINE MONTHS LATER, during the month of September, he was driving his truck hauling heavy logs, when he had a terrible accident and his truck was completely destroyed. Right then, Gregorio heard a voice saying, "I'm calling you to the ministry." Certainly, he must have remembered that 'little piece of paper'.

The following day, he went out to start his other truck, and it wouldn't start. For three months that second truck sat in his yard and wouldn't run. Finally, he sold the truck for $60, explaining to the buyer that it did not work.

To move the truck, the new buyer jump started it and drove it home. Gregory found out later, that the truck worked and continued running for the next three years. It certainly was God's way of working in Gregorio's life and freeing him up for the ministry.

He began his ministry by helping Lowell David's crusade in the city of "La Chorrera", which was close to his home. As we got to know him, we realized he was a good businessman and our Panama City church hired him full-time to manage the construction of the new building.

He finished Bible School, and became part of our staff as Assistant Pastor. When it was time for us to leave Panama and return to the States, the church chose him to become their first Panamanian pastor. This was a church of 1200 people with about 20 outstations, but as assistant pastor he had been well trained. After several years as Pastor, he and his family were sent as missionaries to Ecuador.

HERMINIA VILLAREAL DE HERNANDEZ: PLANTS CHURCH IN THE CITY OF DAVID

Herminia was a believer and a member of another denomination before the Assemblies of God work began in Panama. However, she soon became part of the revival. She studied at the Bible School at night and worked as the secretary of Templo Vista Hermosa during the day. Her secretarial skills were good, but she excelled at answering the phones. She was our best advertisement for the church. She led many people to the Lord over the phone.

Herminia was the young lady who helped Anita and Carmen start the Catholic Charismatic movement in Panama. She was dynamic and without fear in her preaching. She had a tremendous burden for the area of Chiriquí where she was born and for the city of David (Ciudad de David).

The city of David is near the Costa Rican border and about 300 kilometers from Panama City. Several times she spoke to Dick about moving there to start a church.

The Godwins felt led to start a crusade to plant a new church in the city of David. They were warned by other denominations that it was a difficult city. The question was, "Who would go with the Godwins and be the pastor of the new church?" No man wanted to go!

However, knowing of Herminia's desire, it was decided she should be the new pastor. Not everyone was in agreement and some even said, "It probably won't be very large, so what damage can a woman do."

One day, Dick called Herminia into his office and asked her to sit down. "Herminia, I have good news for you. You have been approved to be the pastor of the new work the Godwins will start in David. But, before you say anything, I want to talk to you. Herminia, you are a single lady and it's possible that you will never marry if you become the pastor in David. You could be very lonely. The nearest Assembly of God pastor or church will be five hours away. Some people will never accept a woman pastor, etc., etc."

However, before Dick could finish speaking, Herminia stood to her feet and with fire in her eyes said, "I don't care what it costs me! God has called me and He will be with me!"

The Godwins went to David and put up the tent. Within a short time they had 5,000 attending. God had again sent a revival. A great church was being born.

Now, there were several male workers willing to be the pastor. David Godwin called Dick and said, "What shall we do?" They wisely decided that Herminia had been willing to go, before knowing how large the church would be, and she should be the pastor.

After a few weeks, the Godwins left the new church with Herminia and the hand of the Lord was on her. She soon had a church of several thousand. She started a night Bible School to train workers and eventually started dozens of churches in that area of the country. Again, more beautiful threads were added to the tapestry.

Oh, something important that I need to mention. She did marry and had three children.

You can read more of Herminia's story at the end of this book in the Appendix - under "The Charismatic story in Spain."

THE RICARDO GIRON STORY: FROM STUTTERER TO DYNAMIC PREACHER

Ricardo was one of many young men in our youth group. He sang in the choir, was faithful at church, and loved the Lord. However, he had one small problem. He stuttered when he spoke. Perhaps, because I understood this problem, he became one of my favorites (although I had a lot of favorites).

We left Panama when he was finishing high school. He graduated from the Bible School, and we were thrilled to learn that the Lord had taken away his stuttering.

When Pastor Gregory Campos left to become a missionary in Ecuador, the Panama City church – La Catedral de Vida - choose Ricardo and his wife Silvia as their new pastors.

Ricardo and Silvia have led that great church for over 25 years. Ricardo has also started Christian grade schools and continues to work in Education. Praise the Lord for the great things He has done!

Chapter Eleven: TIME TO LEAVE

It was 1976, and as missionaries it was our time to return to the United States for our year to visit our supporting churches. We had been pastors of La Catedral de Vida for seven years. Dick had almost lost his health and was much in need of rest. By now the church had planted many daughter churches.

It was now time for a Panamanian pastor to take over. God was guiding in all things and we were thrilled when Gregory Campos was voted in as the new pastor.

Campos installed as Pastor

We will always remember January 18, 1976. Two important events took place that day: dedication of the new church building and installation of Gregorio Campos as the new pastor. During the dedication service, Gregorio took his place behind the pulpit and the deacon board and visiting ministers surrounded him. Placing their hands on Gregorio, they prayed for God's anointing and strength to be upon him. Dick told me later that he literally felt the burden of the church lift from his own shoulders and placed on the shoulders of Gregorio Campos. Gregorio and his wife Doris led this great church until God called them to go as missionaries to Ecuador.

Our work was done, but our hearts were forever weaved into the Panamanian tapestry and will be there until eternity. We still go back to visit whenever possible.

The Panamanian youth of our church, Catedral de Vida, were a tremendous influence on our children. We will always be grateful that our children were raised in a church where you could experience miracles and sense the presence of God. They all love and serve the Lord today.

TO PANAMA WITH LOVE

The Bible says that love covers a multitude of sins. That is how my mind works when I think of Panama. I don't remember the heat, the humidity, the extremely hard work, or sickness.

What I remember is the joy of being part of the greatest move of God I have ever experienced. I remember the hunger of the new Christians for the Word of God. I remember how quickly they grew in the things of God and how willingly they said YES to the call for full-time service. I remember believing God would do anything to help us win the world for Christ and then witnessing Him do that very thing.

What faith we had! What passion we had! I will always be grateful for the love and unity between people from different countries, nationalities and cultures. We were united in purpose and love. After most of the founding missionaries had left, the National Church was able to carry on and advance the work because it had been built on the demonstration of the Spirit's power.

CHAPTER TWELVE: AND THE WORK GOES ON

I love the scripture, Acts 13:52, which says that Paul and Barnabas were two happy disciples, brimming with joy and the Holy Spirit.

I'll be the first to say we aren't even a tiny bit like Paul and Barnabas. However, I like to think we are two happy disciples, and I trust, brimming with joy and the Holy Spirit.

We left Panama and went to Madrid, Spain and planted a church with the help of David and Doris Godwin. Our part was small there, but today this church is the largest church in the country of Spain, with daughter churches in many countries. Again, we were only a tiny thread in the tapestry of the work in Spain.

God uses people for special things and special times. I saw the following written but I don't remember who wrote it, "We have completed the work He gave us to do. Soon we'll be in the grave, dust and ashes, but the work goes on.

No Dust and Ashes for the Church of Jesus Christ!

Appendix

THE CHARISMATIC STORY IN SPAIN:
(The rest of herminia's story)

It is awesome to be part of a movement that transcends anything we can plan or organize.

After leaving Panama, the Lord led us to Madrid, Spain to plant a new church. When we arrived in Spain in March 1978, our plan was to begin the crusade in spring or early summer. However, our entire time was spent in going to government offices and completing forms for the necessary permits to put up the tent.

We wanted to become acquainted with the Spanish people and culture. We gladly accepted invitations to visit and to minister in existing evangelical congregations. They were mostly groups of 40 to 60 people who had survived the intense scrutiny and persecution of the years under Franco.

Through mutual friends, we were invited to attend a Charismatic Bible study. We attended two or three meetings and were put on their mailing list.

Weeks later, we received an invitation to attend the first annual Catholic Charismatic Congress to be held in a seminary north of Madrid. We knew the leader of the movement was a Catholic priest, who had contacts with the Notre Dame Renewal movement. We heard he had frequent prayer meetings with Gene Anderson, one of the Assemblies of God missionaries in Barcelona, Spain. Out of curiosity, we decided to attend one or two sessions.

The first session of the Charismatic Congress was an evening meeting during the week. The priests and nuns, who were present, wore "civilian" clothes, so it was difficult to know who was who. I would guess over 1000 people were present. The worship was beautiful. We knew almost all of the worship songs.

During the session, someone gave a prophetic utterance in which the Virgin Mary was mentioned. We were encouraged to follow Mary's advice to "do whatever Jesus says", a reference to her words at the wedding in Cana of Galilee.

I thought it was a very appropriate and biblical expression. However, I could tell that some attendees were a little tense during those moments. When the prophetic utterance was over, one of the female leaders on the platform went to the microphone and began to pray, "Oh Jesus, only you, only you, only you, only you, can save us, can bring us to the Father, can fill us with your Spirit, etc."

(In Spanish, it was so personal and powerful, "solo tú Jesús, solo tú, solo tú") As she repeated that phrase again and again, there was a rising tide of "only you, Jesus, only you, only you, and ¨amén, amén, amén¨ from the crowd. I was amazed and inspired by the intense focus on Christ without in any way denigrating Mary.

The final session of the congress was held on a Sunday afternoon. We attended with our dear friends, **Missionaries David and Doris Godwin**, who had now arrived in Madrid to preach the crusade we were hoping to start. In this session, all the priests and nuns wore their clerical garb. This may have been partly because the Archbishop of Madrid was present.

Again, the worship was beautiful and powerful. There was a deep sense of the presence of God. After the worship, a guest speaker was introduced. He was a priest from the country of Panama. We were surprised and pleased we would be listening to someone from a country that meant so much to all of us.

When the priest from Panama spoke, we realized we were experiencing another one of those connecting miracles, in which the work that God does in one person, often has consequences far beyond anything we could ever imagine.

He told his story of leaving seminary as a disillusioned young priest. Many of his fellow seminarians had accepted Liberation Theology and had gone to various Central American countries to join Marxist rebels. He almost did the same thing, but instead accepted the pastorate of a parish in a small town near David, in the Chiriquí province of Panama.

He celebrated only one mass on Sundays and it was sparsely attended. He became very discouraged. He continued saying, "And then, an American missionary put up a tent in the city of David, provincial capital of Chiriquí."

We looked in amazement at David and Doris Godwin seated next to us. They were the missionaries who had put up that tent!

The priest said that people from his small town went to the tent and came back changed. The town drunk went and came back sober. Marriages were restored, the sick were healed, and many other wonderful transformations happened.

He thought, "I have to go and see what this is all about." He said, "By this time the missionaries had left and a woman was preaching. Can you believe that? A woman!" We knew this woman well; she was our own dear colleague Herminia Villareal.

The priest explained that after attending night after night, his own life was changed. He became convinced of the tremendous power of the simple message of the Gospel. He took notes every night as Herminia preached. Then on Sunday morning, he would lay all those notes on the pulpit of his church and preach from them. Things began to happen. The sick were healed, marriages were restored, and miracles were happening. He had to add a second mass, then a third, and so on.

Finally, in typical Panamanian boldness, he came out from behind the pulpit and looked at the priests who filled the front rows of that great sanctuary. He said, as best we can recall, "Do you call yourself a priest of God? Then stop preaching philosophy or human politics. Preach Jesus Christ in all His glory! Preach the Word of the living God! Preach the Gospel He gave to us! He has not changed and His Word has not changed."

It was one of the most dramatic scenes we have ever witnessed. While he was preaching, we were remembering, years earlier in our church office in Panama City, Herminia with fire in her eyes saying, "Pastor, I don't care what it costs me, I don't care what happens to me, and I don't care how difficult it is. It is what God wants me to do with my life."

Who could have known the significance of that commitment that day? Who could have imagined that even in Spain it would change lives!

After the message, the Archbishop of Madrid was introduced. It was a very solemn moment. He told the crowd he was very tired. The Catholic Church in Spain had just been through the controversial process of deciding what stand to take on the freedom of religion clause in the proposed new democratic constitution.

There had been deep division at the highest levels of the church. He said, "I am going from here to a place of retreat, reflection and rest. I am very tired. But I sense that you who are present here, have something that I need, and I am going to ask the leaders here on the platform to please come and pray for me."

As the charismatic leaders came around and laid hands on the Archbishop, a quiet chorus of prayer went up from the crowd. He was obviously deeply moved.

Again we remembered the words of Herminia, **"I don't care what it costs me pastor...."**

JAN'S STORY

Some have asked to hear my story, and even though it is not in the Spanish version of this book, "Algo Bello", I am adding it here and perhaps it will give more understanding of who I am.

EARLY YEARS

My mother, a city girl, fell in love and married a farmer, but life was hard on their North Dakota farm. These were the dustbowl years. Fields and crops had dried up from the lack of rain. Terrible winds blew across the plains and into every crack and crevice of our house.

My sister, Donna was born in 1935, and I was born in 1939, while World War 2 was raging in Europe. I weighed 11 pounds at birth and my mother could never have any more children. The drought continued and nine months after I was born, my father couldn't make his payments and lost his farm. My mother's relative's kindly helped move us to northern Minnesota.

MY MINNESOTA FARM

Our farm consisted of a small house, garage, barn, outhouse, and 90 acres of land. A windmill turned lazily in the wind as it pumped water from the well. Our dog barked and chased the passing cars on the road in front of the house. Clouds gathering in the west, lightning flashing across the sky and the deep rumble of thunder, brought both blessing and destruction to the crops.

My Dad would strip to the waist out on the back porch and wash up each day when he came in from the fields. His curly black hair glistened with water.

THE AROMA OF BAKING

The aroma of cinnamon rolls baking or my mother canning fruit and vegetables would fill the kitchen. Every afternoon after school my snack was a fried egg mayonnaise sandwich. I'm happy to say my cholesterol still tests low. We always had plenty of food, especially after my father butchered a calf or pig. Because our farm was small, my father also had to work a full time job in the small town nearby.

FLOUR SACK CLOTHES

You could hear the old singer sewing machine whirl as my mother sewed beautiful flour sack dresses for my sister Donna and me. Yes, they really were made from 50 lb. sacks of flour that we brought home from the store. The flour was used for baking and the material, which sometimes was made with colored flowers, actually made very nice dresses and we thought we looked pretty. At least we looked like all the other kids in our one room schoolhouse. My sister Donna was 4 ½ years older than me and when there was money, she would get the new clothes, which were later handed down to me. (At least that is how I remember it.)

DID YOU SAY RUNNING WATER?

There was no running water in the house, so my father was the running water. I can still hear the crunch of his boots in the winter, and see him sinking up to his knees in the snow banks, as he carried his two buckets of water from the well to the house. Every day, every day!

Our family ate together each evening around the dining room table. We were meat and potato people. My mother always made sure that my Dad had the biggest piece of meat. On cold mornings, my sister and I would stand by the potbelly stove in the living room, one on each side as we dressed for school.

At Christmas, our tree stood in front of the living room window and had real burning candles.

MUSIC FILLED OUR HOME

Many nights after dinner, we would gather around the piano to sing and play Christian songs. My Dad would strum his guitar, my mother her mandolin, my sister blew her saxophone and yes, and I tickled the ivories. What a joyful noise we made! Surely you could hear the dog as he howled outside the window!

My parent's bedroom was on the main floor between the kitchen and the living room. I remember my mother kneeling by her bed at night and thanking God for the day. Many times I heard my name mentioned. I wonder if I had I been good or bad that day? My memory fails me.

The second floor, with its slanted roof, is where my sister and I slept. In our room there was a window, which frosted over in the winter. My bed was on the left and her bed was on the right.

TWO SEAT OUTHOUSE

Walking outside, you would see our two- seat outhouse. There was a door, but no electric lights, so we had to leave the door open just a crack, to let the light in. The Sears catalogue was found in the outhouse, but it wasn't just there for reading. We would tear out a page, crunch and wrinkle the paper, and soon it would be soft enough to use on our bottoms. When the temperature dipped below zero, we put a chemical toilet upstairs and again my dad was busy emptying the bucket. In the winter, baths were once a week in the kitchen. We bathed in order, from youngest to the oldest, so I was first in and enjoyed the clean water. In the summer, we carried the tub outside and bathed in the garage.

LOVE IN OUR HOUSE

There was love in our house. I remember seeing my dad come up behind my mother and mischievously untie her apron strings. That was his way of saying "I love you." Each Sunday we climbed into our old car and drove to church as a family. My childhood was an extremely happy time. We were poor, but I didn't know it. It was just life. I now realize how rich we really were.

LOST

An abundance of rain, that summer of 1942, had filled the deep ditches along the roads with water, and the corn grew tall in the fields. My dad was bedridden with Rheumatoid Arthritis and was suffering from the intense heat. On a hot, humid day, when I was only three years old, I wondered away from our farmhouse. My mother, realizing I was missing, called family and friends to help search for me. My Uncle saw something moving in the cornfield across the road from our house. Thinking it might be a dog he walked closer and saw it was my little blond head bobbing up and down in the cornfield. He quickly came, picked me up and carried me home. I was in good condition, except for some scratches on my legs. The big unanswered question in our family has always been "How did Janice get to the cornfield"? "How did she cross that deep ditch of water without falling in and drowning? How did I? I like to think that God heard the prayers of my father. Although unable to get out of bed to help with the search, he must have been praying for my safe return.

ACCEPTING THE LORD

"Mom, will you come forward with me? I want to give my heart to Jesus tonight". Since my birth, I had been taken to church and had been taught about Jesus. One night, when I was six, we drove to a small Baptist Church in Thief River Falls, MN to hear Evangelist Dalzell. At the end of his message he said "If you want to give your heart to Christ, please come forward so I can pray with you." I just knew I had to go forward. My Mother took my hand, we walked to the front of the church, knelt together, and I asked Jesus to come into my heart. As I left the church that night, I felt so clean and free from all my sins. I was six years old and have never turned back.

WORKING WITH MY DAD

On the farm everyone works. My sister Donna helped my mother in the house with the cleaning and cooking. As there was no boy in our family, I became a tomboy, and worked with my father in the barn and fields. When I was nine years old, I learned to drive our shift-stick car. Of course, by then you would find me driving the John Deere tractor and pulling other machinery too.

SPEAKING DIFFICULTIES

Only those who knew me when I was young know what I am telling you now. I doubt if my children even know this. Part of the reason for keeping this secret is that I did not want any of my children or grandchildren to think they had inherited this problem. Thank God they did not.

I don't remember when I started to stutter. In school, when reading out loud, I could hardly get the words out. So many times, I was ashamed and cried. I remember planning how I would say something or choosing what words to use before I started a sentence. On the other hand, I could act in a school play with very few problems. I could sing with no difficulty. I had lots of friends and I spoke well with them. I thank God for the musical talents He gave me, which made it possible for me to be very popular and have many avenues to serve the Lord.

BAPTISM IN THE HOLY SPIRIT

When I received the Baptism in the Holy Spirit, and began speaking in tongues, I sensed a new confidence and began to stutter less. This was during my first year in College. When the Lord called us to be missionaries to Latin America, I knew I would need to learn a new language. I wondered, "How will I ever be able to do that? I have difficulty in just speaking English".

It was at this time that my life verse became Philippians. 4:13: "I can do all things through Christ who strengthens me". I have quoted that verse hundreds of times and God has proved to be faithful. Being confident of our call and holding on to my life verse, I was ready to go.

In language school, the teachers had students repeat a phrase over and over again until we had the right intonation. I was able to do that and eventually learned to speak Spanish, the most beautiful language in the world.

I'm so grateful for Dick who many times saw I was having trouble with my words and would jump in and finish my sentences for me. However, as I often remind him now, "Honey, I don't need your help anymore and I'll be happy to finish my own sentences".

The Lord has brought me so far. I've had the privilege of leading thousands of women in Retreats. Now I'm in my seventies and very rarely think about it anymore except to say "Thank you Lord, for helping me do all things".

MUSICAL PREPARATION

Music has always been a great part of who I am - both singing and playing the piano. My parents could only afford to pay for one year of piano lessons for me, but I had the advantage of learning from my sister Donna, who learned first, and to this day still plays better than I do. Soon, I was playing the piano for Sunday school in our little country church. Also, many Sunday mornings, I would get up early to provide the music for a church radio program. In college, I took organ lessons and eventually I learned to play the vibraharp and the accordion. My dream was to be a minister's wife or an evangelist's wife.

TALL, DARK AND HANDSOME

I was a senior in high school, January 1957, when I saw the man who would become my husband. I was playing the piano at a youth service when I spotted him. Dick was 23 years old and had just returned from three years of military service in the country of Panama. This tall, dark and handsome crew cut man drove a brand new 57 yellow and black hardtop Chevrolet. Wow! I was dating another very nice young man, who drove a 1957 white Ford, but he lived farther away and soon I said goodbye to him.

Dick had accepted the Lord as his Savior while in the army in Panama and was so in love with the Lord. He began to attend the Evangelical Free Church where I attended. I remember him being asked to pray in a service and how he prayed with such authority. He was very bold in the things of the Lord. We continued dating the rest of my senior year. I graduated from High School in June 1957, and that fall, Dick and I went to Bible College in Minneapolis, Minnesota. He attended North Central Bible College while I attended Northwestern. At that time, I worked part-time at the Billy Graham Evangelistic Association.

OUR ENGAGEMENT

It was 20 below zero on the night of Dec. 21, 1957. The stars were shining brightly over the white clean snow. We were driving in the car when Dick pulled over onto a dark road. He stopped the car and turned to me and said, "Let's get out and look at the moon." We got out and walked around to the back of the car. Suddenly, Dick bent over and opened the trunk and took out a small black box. Putting his arms around me, he asked me if I would marry him. I was so excited and of course I said, "Yes". In the light of the beautiful moon, he opened the box, took out the ring and slipped it on my finger. Many times I have teased him that it was so cold outside that I had to say yes in order to get back into the car.

That was the beginning of our life together. Little did I know the excitement that awaited me! My life changed forever and truly it has been **"Something Beautiful"**.

www.ingramcontent.com/pod-product-compliance
Lightning Source LLC
Chambersburg PA
CBHW071016040426
42443CB00007B/807